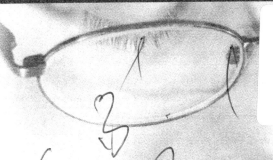

Interpretation
of
DREAMS

VOLUME ONE

KOFI ODURO

KOFI ODURO

INTERPRETATION OF DREAMS

ASEDA PUBLICATIONS

ISBN 97809551355088

INTRODUCTION

The concept of this book is to demystify the mystery that surrounds dreams. There is a huge misconception that accompanies the divinity of dream. There are some people who don't believe in dreams at all, there are some also who believe; if God wants to speak to me in my dreams, why don't I understand them? Why do I forget my dreams? Why does the devil keep using my dreams to cause havoc in my life? And there is another group of people who believe dreams are an avenue through which God communicates to mankind, also it is a medium through which the devil plays gimmicks in the dreamers life.

I want you to understand that dreams are real, they are tangible, and they are effective. I define dreams as a Revelation Gift (The Illumination that passes through the Human Spirit when the person is asleep).

In the Old Testament, God communicated to man through:

1.   Dreams.

2.   Urim

3.   The Prophets.

And when Saul enquired of the Lord, the Lord answered him not, neither by dreams, nor by Urim nor by the prophets. 1Sam.28:6.

Therefore, dreams are tangible to our modern day settings, for edification, direction and restoration to the born again believer. Many don't want anything to do with messages that are wrapped in parenthesis, such as dreams.

For God speaketh once yea twice, yet man percieveth it not. In a dream, in a vision of the night, when deep sleep falleth upon man, in slumberings upon the bed, then he openeth the ears of man, and sealeth their instruction. That he may withdraw; man from his purpose and hide pride from man. He keepeth back his soul from the pit, and his life from perishing by the sword.
Job 33:14-18.

As we learn through a journey of faith in this Book by the help of the Holy Spirit, transformation, transfiguration and translation from glory to glory will take place in your destiny, to stand the test of time and overcome the forces of darkness.

And also posses what is yours from this generation to the coming generations swiftly. Come with me on a journey of faith. It is well, in Jesus name!

3MAJOR DENOMINATION OF DREAMS.

To simplify and accurately understand your dreams, it is expedient to classify them first, and put all the puzzles together and the Holy Spirit will grant you supernatural illumination and enlightenment.

There are three major categories of Dreams, they are:

1.   Direct Dreams.

2.   Symbolic Dreams.

3.   Complex Dreams.

DIRECT DREAM

A direct dream is simply a dream that passes through the spirit or mind of the dreamer and does not need any interpretation whatsoever. Just as you saw in the dream, so is the meaning, whether good or evil (except by divine intervention).

Then Joseph, being a just man and not willing to make her a public example, was minded to put her away privily.

But while he thought on these things, behold the angel of the Lord appeared unto him in a dream, saying Joseph, thou son of David, fear not to take unto thee Mary thy wife for that which is conceived in her is of the Holy Ghost. And she shall bring forth a son and thou shall call His name JESUS; for He shall save his people form their sins.

Now all this was done, that it might be fulfilled which was spoken of the LORD by the prophet, saying, behold a virgin shall be with a child and shall bring forth a son, and they shall call HIS name Emmanuel, which being interpreted is, God with us. Then Joseph being raised from sleep did as the angel of the Lord had bidden him and took unto him his wife. Matthew 1:19-25.

SYMBOLIC DREAMS

A symbolic dream is the illustration of ordinary symbols depicting an actual Apocalypse. Without a thorough, accurate and perfect interpretation of the symbols, the real meaning of a symbolic dream can never be discovered.

The velocity of symbolic dreams in every dreamer's dream is extremely fascinating. The Holy Spirit moves in a manifold domain, and one of the domains of the Spirit of God is the power of symbolism. As far as dreams are concern, symbols and their meanings are very crucial.

Then Daniel, whose name was Belteshazzar, was astonied for one hour, and his thoughts troubled him. The king spake, and said, Belteshazzar, let not the dream, or the interpretation thereof, trouble thee. Belteshazzar answered and said, My lord, the dream be to them that hate thee, and the interpretation thereof to thine enemies. The tree that thou sawest, which grew, and was strong, whose height reached unto the heaven, and the sight thereof to all the earth; Whose leaves were fair, and the fruit thereof much, and in it was meat for

all; under which the beasts of the field dwelt, and upon whose branches the fowls of the heaven had their habitation: It is thou, O king, that art grown and become strong: for thy greatness is grown, and reacheth unto heaven, and thy dominion to the end of the earth. And whereas the king saw a watcher and an holy one coming down from heaven, and saying, Hew the tree down, and destroy it; yet leave the stump of the roots thereof in the earth, even with a band of iron and brass, in the tender grass of the field; and let it be wet with the dew of heaven, and let his portion be with the beasts of the field, till seven times pass over him; This is the interpretation, O king, and this is the decree of the most High, which is come upon my lord the king: That they shall drive thee from men, and thy dwelling shall be with the beasts of the field, and they shall make thee to eat grass as oxen, and they shall wet thee with the dew of heaven, and seven times shall pass over thee, till thou know that the most High ruleth in the kingdom of men, and giveth it to whomsoever he will. And whereas they commanded to leave the stump of the tree roots; thy kingdom shall be sure unto thee, after that thou shalt have known that the heavens do rule.
Dan 4:19-26

COMPLEX DREAMS

Complex dreams are complicated dreams intertwined with numbers, colours, writing, inscriptions, etc. **A complex dream leaves the soul of the dreamer in total confusion.** Complex dreams are complex as the word complex.

When writing, paintings, sketches, drawings, etc. beyond your comprehension begin to manifest and gain roots in your dreams; it leaves seeds of desperation and a quest for understanding in your spirit. It also provokes the margin of your understanding to a point of elasticity.

But by the help of the Holy Spirit, your dream life will be ignited to the "worlds" of Joseph and Daniel today, for a supernatural revolution.

When two full years had passed, Pharaoh had a dream: He was standing by the Nile, when out of the river there came up seven cows, sleek and fat, and they grazed among the reeds. After them, seven other cows, ugly and gaunt, came up out of the Nile and stood beside those on the riverbank. And the cows that were ugly and gaunt ate up the seven sleek, fat cows. Then Pharaoh woke up. He fell asleep again and had a second dream: Seven heads of grain, healthy and good, were growing on a single stalk. After them, seven other heads of grain sprouted--thin and scorched by the east wind. The thin heads of grain swallowed up the seven healthy, full heads. Then Pharaoh woke up; it had been a dream. Gen 41:1-7

10 MINOR
CATEGORIES OF DREAMS

1. SERIAL DREAMS

Serial dreams are sect of "incomplete dreams" that passes through the mind of the dreamer at different conservative times in bits and pieces (at different nights).

And Joseph dreamed a dream, and he told it to his brethren: and they hated him yet the more. <u>And he dreamed yet another dream,</u> and told it to his brethren, and said behold, I have dreamed a dream more; and behold the sun and the moon and the eleven stars made obeisance to me. Genesis 37:5 & 9.

In the above scripture you can see the precipitation of serial dreams. Joseph had the same dream spread on different occasions in parts or in phases, therefore he told it to his brothers on different times as the serial dreams unfolded. **Most Christians keep receiving divine revelations from the Holy Spirit in a serial dimension, this helps you to comprehend or understand the message God is conveying to you systematically. <u>Prophetic messages come in</u>**

sequence. God releases divine information in a sequential order to help the modern day Christian to fathom it gradually. Therefore serial dreams are legitimate to your Christian life.

2.   DREAMS OF REVELATION TO REDEMPTION

These are the kind of dreams God uses as a channel of deliverance to deliver his people from the atrocity and conspiracies of the devil and to establish his eternal counsel.

And when there arose a great dissension, the chief captain, fearing lest Paul should have been taken by force from among them, and to bring him into the castle. And the night following the Lord stood by him, and said, be of good cheer, Paul: for as thou hast testified of me in Jerusalem, so must thou bear witness also at Rome. Acts 23:10-11.

Most dreams fall into the category of revelation to redemption. **God reveals to redeem!** Let the devil do his worst in your dreams, but the best of Gods outstretched arm of redemption and deliverance will definitely be your potion for good and not for evil. May your nightmares be turned into revelations to redemption, and may woes in the night be turned into celebration in Jesus mighty name! Amen!

3.   PROGRESSIVE DREAMS

Progressive dreams are supernatural revelations that predict the dreamer's elevation and favourable promotion. They are positive dreams; They are good dreams!

And the chief butler told his dream to Joseph, and said to him in my dream, behold, a vine was before me and in the vine were three branches; and it was as though it budded, and her blossoms shoot forth; and the clusters thereof brought forth ripe grapes; And pharaoh's cup was in my hands. And Joseph said unto him, this is the interpretation; three branches are three days, yet within the three days, shall pharaoh lift up thine head, and restore thee unto thy place; and thou shall deliver pharaoh's cup into his hand, after the formal manner where thou wast his butler. Genesis 40:9-13.

This category of dreams serves as a telescopic gaze into the dreamer's future. The butler's dream is a progressive dream; it unveils untapped potentials in your life by the Holy Spirit of God. Progressive dreams are boosters to your faith. It encourages you to know that there is hope for your future. I trust that your dreams, as a child of God will be in the domain of progressive dreams.

4.   RETROGRESSIVE DREAMS

Retrogressive dreams are a bunch of negative and disastrous dreams the devil uses to abort the legitimate success of the dreamer. These dreams are a company of setback dreams.

When the chief baker saw that the interpretation was good, he said to Joseph, I also was In my dream, and, behold I had three white baskets on my head: and in the uttermost basket there was all manner of bakements for pharaoh and the birds did eat them out of the basket upon my head. And Joseph answered and said, this is the interpretation thereof: the three baskets are three days: yet within three days shall pharaoh lift up your

*head from off thee, and shall hang thee on a tree; and the
birds shall eat thy flesh from off thee.
Genesis 40:16-19.*

I am thrilled at the prolific interpretation Joseph
gave to this retrogressive dream! The scripture
above is an excellent definition of a retrogressive
dream. Retrogressive dreams are the terrain of
Satan against the dreamer, to malign,
marginalize, castigate, antagonize, complicate,
frustrate and pull the dreamer down completely.
But the devil is already defeated! God will
frustrate his efforts, and the almighty Father will
come through for you, amen!

5.   INSIGHT DREAMS

Insight dreams are the class of dreams that flashes
through the spirit of the dreamer whiles sleeping,
and predicts events, times, programs and the
eternal council of God for your present moment.

*Then spake the Lord to Paul in the night by a vision (a
dream), be not afraid but speak, hold not thy peace, for*

readiness of what the lord will be doing in your life, based on what you've seen in your dreams.

And Joseph said unto pharaoh, the dream of pharaoh is one, God has showed pharaoh what he was about to do. Genesis 41:25.

God is the revealer of all mysteries! Kenneth Hagan wrote in many of his books that, the Holy Spirit would reveal to him in a dream, a forth coming healing and miracle service, and what He will be doing in the meetings. And the next day really in the meeting, it would be the exact replication of what he saw in his dream, amazing isn't it?

Many Christians can remark of this experience, seeing an event in your dream before it manifest. I pray that you will see your season of elevation before it manifest, in Jesus mighty name!

7. INTERCESSORY DREAMS

So many dreamers are intercessors by God's

*am with thee, and no man shall set on thee to hurt thee:
For I have much people in this city. Acts 18:9-10.*

Insight dreams declares the mind of God to the dreamer, what God thinks of the situation at stake. For instance, if a young lady is caught up in a dilemma of the proposal of marriage of two gentlemen, the Holy Spirit through insight dreams will distinguish between them both, and let the lady know the right one. Many modern day Christians have attained God's "circum-navigation" (all-round prophetic direction), at very crucial moments of their lives through insight dreams. So you see, dreams in general are very powerful avenues of spiritual communication!

6. FORESIGHT DREAMS

Foresight dreams are visionary predictions, advance knowledge, and prophetic canticles of the Holy Ghost, which he reveals to a dreamer, long before they happen. Foresight dreams quickens your prayer life and puts you in divine calling. God has given the ability of dreams to dreamers as a channel of deliverance to deliver many. As a matter of fact when you dream of other people, the purpose is to intercede on their behalf or to stand in the gab for them in prayer. Seeing friends and loved ones in your dreams being attacked by "alien forces", being abused, in trouble, in pain, in tears, at the graveyard , in the hospital, in the mortuary, in need etc. calls for urgent prayer, before the situation gets out of hand. Make use of the intercessory gift over your life, by calling on Jehovah God in fervent and spirit filled prayers, to swiftly rescue the people at stake!

Many pastors intercede for their members through intercessory dreams. Waste no time when you dream about other people. And don't be in rush to tell them. But as God has revealed to you in your dream, intercede for them. It may be an individual, a group of people, a ministry or even a nation.

In the first year of the reign of Darius, I Daniel understood by the books the number of years, whereof

the word of the lord came to Jeremiah the prophet, that he would accomplish seventy years in the desolation of Jerusalem. <u>And I set my face unto the Lord God to seek by and supplications, with fasting and sackcloth and ashes</u>:
Daniel 9:2-3.

Daniel set his face to pray and to intercede for the people of Israel and to seek the mercy of God for a people that were in captivity, after an intriguing revelation.

8.   ESCATOLOGICAL DREAMS

Escatology is the study of the end-times. Prophetic events, happenings, orchestrations of the last days and things that must take place before the world comes to an end, normally, it consists of the second coming of our Lord Jesus, the Judgment day etc. Most dreamers see this very often. God normally communicate to dreamers to caution them of the coming days of tribulation, to save themselves and others. When you encounter any of the following dreams, the

Spirit of God is hammering on the core or the pivot of the end-times: seeing the world coming to a close, the sun, moon, stars falling, the mountains melting, lightings, thundering, strong winds, tornados, people running for their dear lives, etc and etc. These dreams are real, they are not a myth. Take precaution, and act now!

"And he said, behold, <u>I will make thee know</u> what shall be in the last end of the indignation: for at the appointed time the end shall be." Daniel 8:19.

9. PATTERNED DREAMS

Pattern dreams are continual repetition of either negative or positive train of dreams that have effectual impacts on the dreamer's destiny.

When he was set down on the judgment seat, his wife sent unto him, saying have thou nothing to do with that just man, I have suffered many things this day in a dream because of him. Matt 27:19.

The emphasis made on "many things" in the above mentioned scripture cannot be underestimated. It means that the dream of the wife of Pontius Pilate was continuous in phases, highlighted, and repetitious. Some people encounter negative pattern in their dreams, others a positive pattern of dreams and some too, both. <u>A dream can be classified as a pattern dream when it follows the same trend for a long time.</u> Prayerful reaction and investment must be made to correct the negative pattern of your dreams before the situation gets out of control. It is never the will of God to suffer a negative trend in your dreams; rather it is a deliberate diabolic intention of the devil to frustrate you and to destroy your God given future. Face it! Take dominion!

10. IMAGINARY DREAMS

When you normally sleep with your television, radio, mp3, i pod, or any audible set on, you are likely to have an imaginary dream. <u>An imaginary dream is a visual collection of thoughts that dominates your spirit, when you sleep with any</u>

of the above mentioned sets on. For instance, if you sleep with your radio set on, you may dream and see yourself in that radio station, or anything associated with radio. Imaginary dreams are baseless! They don't have interpretations and they don't have effects! They are also not common. It happens once in a hundred. Don't try understanding an imaginary dream, it is just a cluster of imaginations that flips through your mind whiles trying to catch some sleep. Please don't misinterpret a complex dream for an imaginary dream. Be led by the Holy Ghost to distinguish between the two.

UNDERSTANDING SYMBOLS AND TOKENS.

There are numerous symbolic epiphanies in the bible. The books of Daniel and Revelation are real proofs. The bible itself is a great mystery. The journey with God and the work of ministry is a package of faith. To understand "coded language", divine symbols, tokens, emblems, and signs, it is the work of the Holy Spirit.

The apostle Paul was caught up to heaven whiles still alive. John the beloved disciple of Christ was lifted to heaven from the island of Patmos, and he saw revelations of God, Can you imagine if they lacked the ability and potential to comprehend what God revealed to them? Receive this same potential and more to do exploits according to the power that works in you, for it is God who works in you both to will and to do His good pleasure!

To understand "coded language", divine symbols, tokens, emblems, and signs, it is the work of the Holy Spirit.

I commend you to God and to the word of his grace, which is able to build you up and to give

an inheritance in Christ Jesus. Acts 20:32

The following are apocalyptic chronicles the Holy Spirit has embedded into my spirit to share with you.

Symbols
AND INTERPRETATION
POSITIVE SYMBOLS
EGGS :- POTENTIALS

The bible says "how small a whisper we have heard of God, but the thunder of his power who can understand?" Job26:14b.

As God has implanted rich mineral resources in the belly of the earth, so has He stored exceptional and exquisite talents, gifts, abilities, and potentials in mankind. God reveals these treasures which dwell in earthen vessels to mankind sometimes in their dreams. An egg in your dream stands for your potential (your power to produce or to manufacture, and to bring forth).

> **Interpretation**
> *Eggs portray Favourable opportunities of a dreamer's destiny and future.*

Eggs portray Favourable opportunities of a dreamer's destiny and future. When you see, handle or taste them in dreams. It represents the potentials of a Great person. If you are trusting God for fertility or fruitfulness in every facet of your life, and you happen to dream of eggs, it means potency or potentials.

Functional Prophetic Declaration:
My Father and my God, in the name of Jesus I invoke every destined arrangement you have made for my life. I inhabit it without struggle, and I declare that any symbolic encounter with eggs in my dreams shall be made manifest with immediate effect.

Scriptural Infusion
See, I am doing a new thing! Now it springs up; do you not perceive it? I am making a way in the wilderness and streams in the wasteland. Isaiah 43:19. (NIV)

KEYS:- AUTHORITY

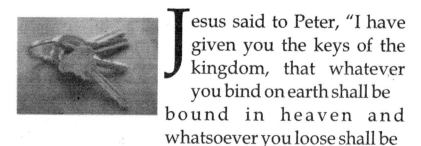

Jesus said to Peter, "I have given you the keys of the kingdom, that whatever you bind on earth shall be bound in heaven and whatsoever you loose shall be loosed." The revelation here is the Keys! The keys of the kingdom are the authority of the kingdom. When a key or a bunch of keys are being handed over to you, or you use a key, or work in the locksmiths, etc; it means divine authority released into your spirit for fortification. This authority is rear, it comes from God, and it is pure, holy and effective. I believe this kind of authority is the anointing that comes on a person and makes him/her do the impossible. Keys in your Dreams represent authority or access. The illustration to prevail over a situation after a time of spiritual warfare and travail has been embellished into the emblem of keys by God in your dreams.

Interpretation

Keys in your Dreams represent authority or access.

Functional Prophetic Declaration:
Father you are a God of possibilities, sovereignty and authority; I pronounce the coming of your infallible power and access into my daily life for the rest of time into eternity. I call for a heavenly back-up to establish your judicial council for my life in Jesus mighty name, amen.

FRUITS: -GIFTS

Most dreamers on a regular bases see diverse kinds of fruits in their dreams. It's a great joy to encounter the harvest of fruits, the seeds, and even the growth process of fruits. Fruits such as, mangoes pineapples, pear, passion fruit, oranges, guava, grapes, berries; apples, etc. can be seen in your dreams. All these and more, represents Gifts! Spiritual gifts, intellectual gifts and creative gifts. Gifts for the ministry, for

Interpretation
All these and more, represents Gifts! Spiritual gifts, intellectual gifts and creative gifts.

your career or profession, for the running of your home, for governance, for innovation and inventions, etc.

The moment you begin to have these dreams, acknowledge the real truth that you have found favour with God and with men. The Lord will begin to announce you to your generation quickly, by the time you know, you are already at the top and at the front line doing exploits by the grace of God in your generation!

Functional Prophetic Declaration:

Thank you heavenly Father, for empowering me heavily with spiritual, prudential, and creative power and instincts. I speak prophetically to every virtue and treasure of God within me to comply vividly and precisely with the perfect will of God in the mighty name of Jesus the Christ.

Scriptural Infusion

This is why it says: "When he ascended on high, he took many captives and gave gifts to his people." Eph 4:8 (NIV)

HORIZON: -YOUR DUE SEASON

The elegance of nature or Gods creative works is tremendous and awesome. And that is one of the reasons why God chooses simple things around us to depict or represent an actual concept. Seasons come and seasons go, but when a dreamer's season is approaching, one of the symbols that will follow pattern is the symbol of a Horizon. A dreamer's season will reflect in his / her dream as a colourful horizon. Horizon simply means where the skies meet with the sea or the land. Recognise immediately by the help of the Holy Spirit that your season is due, once you begin to see new Horizon's in your dreams or visions. Life can get better and better if your dreams follow

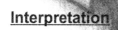

Interpretation

Recognise immediately by the help of the Holy Spirit that your season is due, once you begin to see new Horizon's in your dreams or visions.

this suite. Joseph the dreamer had a dream and he told it to his brothers, and the bible says he had yet another dream, the second dream, was a confirmation of his season of elevation. The symbols of that dream was connected to insulations, horizon and the galaxies. Invest more prayer into such dreams for transformation.

Functional Prophetic Declaration:
All creation are witnesses that I am a product of the spontaneous spoken word of God (rhema), born in such a time like this to fulfill divine mandate and obligation. I pronounce in Jesus name that every appearance of Horizon in my dreams shall come to pass as intended by Jehovah God in Jesus name!

Scriptural Infusion
"Arise, shine, for your light has come, and the glory of the LORD rises upon you. Isaiah 60:1 (NIV)

MIRROR:- A PICTURE OF YOUR FUTURE

Naturally a mirror is an admirable element, when you stand before it to behold yourself in it. The mirror reflects to you your real image. But the interesting thing is that spiritually, a mirror has a far better meaning and significance.

Interpretation

The meaning of a mirror in your dreams reveals what will become of you in the future and the intentions of God towards you.

The meaning of a mirror in your dreams reveals what will become of you in the future and the intentions of God towards you. God downloads destiny information into your spirit far before it happens. Don't take such dreams as "one of those dreams;" but pursue them prayerfully for greatness. Seeing yourself standing before a mirror, dressing yourself, wearing nice cloths, dressing your hair, etc. is a telescopic gaze into your future.

Sometimes it may not be yourself but other people, who will be in the mirror. When you see other people in your dreams posing in a mirror, it means a picture of their future. God is revealing to you that he will elevate them.

Functional Prophetic Declaration:

Dear God, Almighty and everlasting Father, I humbly ask you to proof yourself in my destiny, lift me to where I belong, and let all eyes see your kindness adorning me in the presence of my adversaries. Guarantee my future for good and not for evil. It is established through Jesus Christ my Lord, amen.

Scriptural Infusion

For I know the plans I have for you," declares the LORD, "plans to prosper you and not to harm you, plans to give you hope and a future.
Jeremiah 29:11. (NIV).

CROWN:- FAVOUR OF GOD

The bible says "Isaac planted in the year of famine, and God favoured him and he became great, and he grew and became greater, and went forward until he became very great." That is the favour of God, His unmerited grace. Many great people received measures of supremacy through massive deposits of Gods favour, in their dreams. A crown in your dreams means the favour of God. Whether it is a royal crown, pageantry crown, or an honorary crown, the meaning is the same. When you see a crown, handle a crown, being given a crown or being crowned in a dream, it means that your destiny has just been accessed into the fullness of God's favour and acceptance. Also if you loose your crown in a dream you have lost the favour of God. If the dream is an intercessory, and in case

Interpretation

A crown in your dreams means the favour of God.

God reveals an individual, a church, or even a nation, loosing a crown or other significant symbols of the same meaning, then the urgency of prayer must be enforced for restitution of the favour of God.

Functional Prophetic Declaration:

Lord I bless you for your favour upon my life, I am so excited that dreams like these imprint and embellish your favour into my spirit. I trust that with this favour, my legacy will be indelible and contagious, and I will be a blessing to generations even unto posterity in Jesus powerful name!

Scriptural Infusion

'He will wipe every tear from their eyes. There will be no more death' or mourning or crying or pain, for the old order of things has passed away."
Rev. 21:4. (NIV) .

FLAMES:-THE ANOINTING

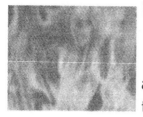

There are many symbols for the anointing. One of them is Flames! Blazes are very powerful and crucial in the dreams of every child of God who has a quest for the anointing. This brings us to the real meaning of flames in our dreams. Flames represents the anointing, the unction, the ovation of the power of God. If you are in the ministry or you have just been called into the ministry, encountering dreams of this fashion, catapults you to another altitude in your walk with God. The visitation of the Holy Spirit is embedded into such dreams. It is meant to motivate you, inspire you, strengthen and empower you for the work of the ministry and the edification of the body of Christ. I know some people who have received the baptism of the Holy Spirit and the baptism of fire when they dreamt of different colours of flames.

> **Interpretation**
> *flames represents the anointing, the unction, the ovation of the power of God.*

There are three kinds of Flames every dreamer must understand;

1.   Yellow flames- signifies the anointing   of the Holy Spirit over an individual's life for a purpose.

2.   Green Flames- highlights unction of the Holy Spirit over a group of people, a ministry or a business. This kind of Anointing can also be known as "co-operate anointing."

3.   Blue Flames- are the hottest of all flames. The climatic viscosity ratio of this kind of flames is unspeakable and indisputable. Any dreamer who experience's this magnitude of flames in their dream will climb the highest peak of the anointing and work gigantic exploits of the Holy Ghost.

Functional Prophetic Declaration:
Messiah, let the blazes of your Holy Ghost explode over my ministry and precipitate

exceptional works of God in my life. I ask for an original flow and move of the spirit that cannot be comprehended or fathom. Use me in a spectacular way for your glory even life forevermore, in the name of He that died and rose again, even the Lord Jesus.

Scriptural Infusion

When my path was drenched with cream and the rock poured out for me streams of olive oil. Job 29:6. (NIV)

SWORD:- COMMANDING AUTHORITY

When the storm raged against the disciples of Jesus on the sea, they woke him up lamenting, "rabbi don't you care that we are in trouble"? Then the bible said He got up and rebuked the storm, and drastically there was calm. That is what I call "commanding authority."

The realm of the spirit is complaint to such "commanding authority" without any arguments. A sword, a chopper, knife, spear, dagger, or any sharp, long object for battle in your dreams stands for God's commanding authority. When you receive a sword or use a sword in a dream for any purpose, it reveals the mandate, victory and power the Holy Spirit has bestowed upon you to exercise over your adversaries. Also, in your dream if an opponent or your enemy attacks you with any of these objects, it simply means a satanic sabotage against you success. As a child of God, during a prayer retreat, if you dream or have a vision of any of the above mention objects, it absolutely means an irrefutable authority. This assures you of the help of God.

Interpretation

A sword, a chopper, knife, spear, dagger, or any sharp, long object for battle in your dreams stands for God's commanding authority.

Functional Prophetic Declaration:

I am that child of God whom creation is awaiting with earnest expectations, I cannot fail my generation, and I cannot miss my target. I refuse to settle for less, I reject mediocrity, I will respond positively and responsibly to the charge of God for my life for this generation and generations yet unborn. I will compete with this secular world and proof them wrong, and i will let the world know that horses and chariots are prepared for battle, nevertheless, victory and absolute triumph comes from the Lord!

Scriptural Infusion

Every warrior's boot used in battle and every garment rolled in blood will be destined for burning, will be fuel for the fire. Isaiah 9:5. (NIV)

BREAD:- LOGOS/RHEMA WORD OF GOD

T he bible teaches in parenthesis or in parables the essence of bread as the word of God. This mystery is also applicable with the concept of dreams and visions. Bread in your dreams, means God's prophetic word that metamorphoses your destiny from one level to greater levels. If you are believing God for a miracle, such dreams are spring boards. God's prophetic word comes in two dimensions, Logos and Rhema. (In Greek) 'Logos' is the written and documented word of God. 'Rhema' is the spontaneous, audible spoken word of God. When you bake, sell, eat, give or being given bread in your dreams, it is the momentum of God's word for your life, to give

Interpretation

Bread in your dreams, means God's prophetic word that metamorphoses your destiny from one level to greater levels.

40

you peace and bring you to an expected end. Don't treat these dreams lightly; pursue them in prayer and faith until they manifest to the glory of God the Father, the Son and the Holy Spirit.

Functional Prophetic Declaration:

What is written is written! In the name of Jesus I declare every symbolic appearance of God's prophetic word concerning me will gain pre-eminence hastily and shall come to pass. The season has changed in my favour and interest; I will not be hindered nor restricted in the name of Jesus. I hold my prophetic word into manifestation. I declare all is well with me.

Scriptural Infusion

Then Jesus declared, "I am the bread of life. Whoever comes to me will never go hungry, and whoever believes in me will never be thirsty. John 6:35. (NIV).

A UNICORN IN YOUR DREAMS:- HONOURABLE ELEVATION

If your dreams follow a positive pattern, there are so many wonderful encounters you can experience. Many dreamers have encountered heavenly beings visiting them in their dreams. One of these exceptional symbols you can experience in your dreams is the appearance of a unicorn in your dreams. A unicorn means an honourable elevation. In other words the dreamer has reached a turning point in life. A point of a "sweat free life", at this point God begins to command His blessings in every facet of the dreamer's life. In your low estate in life, the spirit of God can revolutionalize your situation with a dream of a unicorn to encourage you that, the situation will change through an honourable and miraculous elevation.

Interpretation

A unicorn means an honourable elevation.

Functional Prophetic Declaration:
Father, since promotion does not come from the east nor from the west, but you are the judge, you lift up one and set down another, I prophesy in the name of Jesus, that you accelerate me into my honourable elevation. Let my eyes see the miraculous from now and beyond, I position myself strategically under an open heaven for supernatural results, amen.

Scriptural Infusion

You have exalted my horn like that of a wild ox; fine oils have been poured on me. Psalm 92:10. (NIV).

CAKE:- FULFILLMENT OF GOD'S PROPHETIC WORD.

The prophetic ministry is one of the most prolific moves of God, which human mentality cannot fathom. Prophecies, visions and dreams dwell in the same domain. Every Christian is excited to receive an undiluted word from God. But sometimes it is confusing to be kept in suspense, waiting for a prophetic word to manifest.Cake is the spiritual symbol for the fulfilment of God's prophetic word over ones life. In real life, if a dreamer has been trusting God for fulfilment of a word that has been spoken over his/her life, and at the same time, he/she dreams of cake, God will change the situation suddenly and manifest his word to that dreamer. Baking, eating, selling or being given a cake in your dream, announces the fulfilment of God's prophetic word over your life without anymore delay. That's a powerful experience!

> **Interpretation**
> *Cake is the spiritual symbol for the fulfilment of God's prophetic word over ones life.*

Functional Prophetic Declaration:
Eternal Holy Spirit of God, I ask you with meekness to usher me and my family into our prophetic fulfilment. We ask your divine leadership to transfigure every word of yours

concerning us into flesh and show us your glory once more, in Jesus name, amen.

Scriptural Infusion

The LORD said to me, "You have seen correctly, for I am watching to see that my word is fulfilled."
Jeremiah 1:12. (NIV).

SURGERY/OPERATION:- SUPERNATURAL DELIVERANCE

Ayoung professional footballer shared his dream with me recently, and said "I had a dream after a severe injury. In my dream I saw an angel of the Lord by my bedside with a brand new human bone in his hand. The angel started to operate on me; he cut my leg open, removed the old bone and fixed a new one. He smiled and disappeared. I woke up the next morning to physically discover that my leg injury had been healed miraculously". Wow! What a visitation! Surgery or being operated

Interpretation

Surgery or being operated upon in a dream is the highest form of deliverance a dreamer can encounter.

upon in a dream is the highest form of deliverance a dreamer can encounter. Such a surgery in your dream can be in a hospital's operating theatre, labour ward, etc

See, it is God who created you and formed the members of your body and therefore He alone has extra parts. Ironically, the Holy Ghost will visit and deliver you in a state of infirmity, trouble or pain, by operating upon you in a divine dream. God guarantees his children timely intervention. He wipes the tears from your eyes. He puts a new song in your mouth and makes you smile again. Anytime you are in a hospital environment or in a process of therapy in your dream, don't be quick to rule it as a negative dream. Be led by the Holy Spirit.

Functional Prophetic Declaration:
God, once you have spoken twice we have heard that all power belongs to you; I enforce my divine privileges in the name of Jesus right here, right

now. Deliverance is mine in the name of Jesus.

Scriptural Infusion

But on Mount Zion will be deliverance; it will be holy, and the house of Jacob will possess its inheritance. Obadiah 1:17. (NIV).

SHOES:-DOMINION IN LIFE

Every believer fight's for a firm establishment in life. As a matter of fact that is the essence of the cross. Jesus gave us back what Satan took from Adam in the Garden of Eden. Dominion is very crucial to every modern day believer. One of the most essential tokens you can usually see in your dreams are pair of shoes, boots, slippers, sandals, etc. When you see these emblems in your dreams, it highlights dominion, authority, or a firm foundation in life. Let me put it in plain words, as you keep on dreaming about shoes, it clearly means, it is well with you, in terms of a definite success in life. In addition to that, if you dream and you are not wearing shoes it means the opposite. That the viscosity of dominion upon your life as child of God is being challenged by the devil, and that can be devastating, if you

> ### Interpretation
> *pair of shoes, boots, slippers, sandals, etc. when you see these emblems in your dreams, it highlights dominion authority, or a firm foundation in life.*

don't handle it well in prayer. If you wear good and nice looking shoes, with very wonderful apparel in your dream, you have been empowered for exploits and the favour of God is with you for good and not for evil.

Functional Prophetic Declaration:

Lord Jesus, thank you for the work of redemption on the cross of Golgotha, I take my place of dominion, I step into my domain of rule and I refuse to be entangled with any yoke of bondage. I declare that I will exercise this dominion in my daily Christian life to your glory by the power of the Holy Spirit, amen and amen.

CROSSING A BRIDGE:- TRANSITION FROM GLORY TO GLORY

Some symbols have positive or negative meanings depending on how you see them and also the kind of situation that faces you in real life at the time of the dream. To cross a bridge in your dream means to be translated or transformed from one condition to another. When you see a bridge in your dream it signifies that your prayer has attained God's kind reception and change. Sometimes in life you go through

Interpretation
When you see a bridge in your dream it signifies that your prayer has attained Gods kind reception and change.

challenges and in the midst of it when you dream of seeing a bridge, crossing a bridge, approaching a bridge, or driving on a Bridge; the Grace of God catapults you from the challenges into your VICTORY.

Many dreamers have received the help and push of the Holy Spirit into divine rest through these dreams. It is wonderful for your dream to follow a pattern like this. Peradventure, you see other people in your dreams crossing, approaching, or driving on a bridge, it is a prophetic revelation from God through you to them to revolutionalize their situation for the better. I have come across people who just by seeing a bridge, in their dream have been metamorphosed to higher heights. I trust that help will come to you in Jesus Mighty Name.

Functional Prophetic Declaration:

In Jesus name I belong to the top, it can only get better for me and my family, it cannot get worse. I pronounce the victory of God from glory to glory, grace to grace, from wealth to wealth, from abundance unto abundance, and from covering to covering upon my life in Jesus mighty name, amen.

> Scriptural Infusion
> For those God foreknew he also predestined to be con-formed to the image of his Son, that he might be the firstborn among many brothers and sisters. And those he predestined, he also called; those he called, he also justified; those he justified, he also glorified.
> Romans 8:29-30.(NIV).

FLOWERS:- GLORY/FAVOUR OF GOD

In God's infinite Wisdom, flowers, has been designed to beautify and to decorate. Its spiritual meaning differs slightly. If you see flowers, receive flowers, plant flowers, decorate with flowers or harvest flowers in your

Interpretation
. *If you see flowers, receive flowers, plant flowers, decorate with flowers or harvest flowers in your dreams, it means the Glory or the favour of God.*

dreams, it means the Glory or the favour of God. The Holy Spirit will always show you the picture of your destiny and also the road map to the big picture. That is why so many dreamers keep seeing divers' colours of flowers in their dreams. Even though the principal meaning of flowers in your dreams is the favour of God upon your life, the colours of the flowers are also very crucial. I will be sharing with you later in the volume two this book, the meaning of colours in your dreams. Some preachers have misinterpreted this particular symbol to be a symbol of death. But it is not true. Flowers depict the Glory of God over the dreamer's life forevermore.

Functional Prophetic Declaration:
I release the favour of God that came upon Esther, Daniel, Ruth, Joseph, Hannah and Paul into my life. In the name of Jesus I spill the beauty of the Lord God into every facet of my life throughout the rest of time.

Scriptural Infusion
He has made everything beautiful in its time.
He has also set eternity in the human heart; yet

> no one can fathom what God has done from beginning to end. I know that there is nothing better for people than to be happy and to do good while they live.
> Eccl. 3:12-13.(NIV).

NICE CARS:- BUSINESS &FINANCIAL PROGRESS

Cars are very relevant as far as dreams and its interpretations are concerned. There are many people who don't know how to drive in real life, but can see themselves driving perfectly in their dreams. This is fascinating to many dreamers! It doesn't necessarily mean you will be driving a car, but categorically, anytime you dream of sitting in a car, driving a car, buying a

Interpretation

anytime you dream of sitting in a car, driving a car, buying a car or having in your possession a sleek looking car, it means flourishing business, wealthy investments and financial progress.

car or having in your possession a sleek looking car, it means flourishing business, wealthy investments and financial progress. That actually means the dew of Heaven has reached your business and finances for good. The range of cars is also a very important factor for accurate interpretation to your dreams. A salon luxurious car means wealth. Buses or lorries means abundance. Trucks and heavy duty cars means covenant prosperity. Mainly, if you drive, join or even own them, states your financial inheritance in the land of the living. These dreams produce wealth and deposits substance into the spirit of the dreamer and match him/her into unlimited proof of God's blessing. Many times, we misunderstand such dreams and therefore misapply our prayer focus. I pray that God will grant you revelation knowledge to ascend your place allocated to you by God Almighty.

Functional Prophetic Declaration:
God, you are my father and I am your child, your word say's you have given unto me great and mighty promises, and all things that pertains to life and godliness. I believe in the totality of your

word, I speak to wealth to hear the word of the Lord, that from this moment forth, I am very wealthy in Jesus mighty name, amen.

Scriptural Infusion

Instead of bronze I will bring you gold, and silver in place of iron. Instead of wood I will bring you bronze, and iron in place of stones. I will make peace your governor and well-being your ruler.
Isaiah 60:17.(NIV).

GOLD / DIAMONDS:- MAJESTIC WEALTH

This is my favourite symbol in dreams, the moment you encounter them you thrive, you excel and you become "another person". Precious minerals and metals represent God's royal majestic wealth and financial breakthrough. Periodically when you go through hostility and obscurity, your turning point begins when you see gold, diamonds, jasper, onyx, etc. it can be in a form of, gold chains, bracelets, rings, anklets, earrings, crowns or in their row state. Prosperity, abundance and multiplicity of breakthroughs will be the results when you dream of buying, mining, selling or using Gold, Diamonds and any other precious minerals.

Interpretation

. Precious minerals and metals represent God's royal majestic wealth and financial breakthrough.

When people give you these ornaments as gifts in your dreams, it means you are elevated for greater works. I have seen paupers and 'nobody's' become controllers of wealth just by beholding, using, trading, or being adorned with these prospering materials in their dreams. When you discern your dreams are taking this route, determine to convert these powerful revelations of the Holy Spirit into reality in the name of the Son of the living God. I see you thriving, I see you limitless, and I see merchandise of greatness coming to you with speed, and forces of the gentiles as your possession.

Functional Prophetic Declaration:

Father I thank you that poverty, scarcity, struggles and lack has no place in my life. I am liberated by the power of the Holy Spirit in Jesus name. By these dreams I walk in abundance. My store house shall overflow, and my family will walk in God's majestic wealth, in the mighty name of Jesus, amen.

Scriptural Infusion

The least of you will become a thousand, the smallest a mighty nation. I am the LORD; in its time I will do this swiftly." Isaiah 60:22.(NIV).

RAINBOW:- GOD'S MANIFOLD BLESSING

God in the days of Noah sworn not to destroy creation with flood again. The bible says He sealed it with the sign of the rainbow. A rainbow is a formation of cloud in the skies, which has many colours in it. It appears in the skies periodically and disappears. Any time you see this sign in you dream it show the versatility of the blessings of God in your life. The rainbow in dreams means different forms of God's blessing at a time. In other words, an unstoppable, unrestricted, irrevocable, unchangeable blessing that comes from the throne of God to substitute your wilderness experience. Just as the colours of the rainbow are many and elegant, so are the blessings that accompany it. Dignity and Greatness will suddenly hit you when you dream of seeing the rainbow, being surrounded by the rainbow or encountering the occurrence of a Rainbow. Most of the divine visitations most Christians encounter in their dreams have got to do with rainbow and other divine symbols. In the days of Noah the rainbow was God's turning point for man, in the same way in your dreams, it is God's turning point for you!

Interpretation
The rainbow in dreams means different forms of God's blessing at a time.

Functional Prophetic Declaration:

I am a candidate of miracles! Divers kinds of miracles are part of my life! And I am fully blessed! I am not cursed; I don't accept curses in my life! Every follicle, fibre and texture of my being is a manifold blessing from the Lord. Praise God!

Scriptural Infusion

The LORD will grant you abundant prosperity — in the fruit of your womb, the young of your livestock and the crops of your ground — in the land he swore to your ancestors to give you. The LORD will open the heavens, the store-house of his bounty, to send rain on your land in season and to bless all the work of your hands. You will lend to many nations but will borrow from none.

Deut. 28:11-12.(NIV).

GALAXY / STARS / SUN / MOON:-
GREATNESS AND PROMINENCE.

The Excellency of your Dignity and the beauty of your destiny are encapsulated in the above mentioned symbols in your dream. The essence of stars, the moon, the sun and other installations in your dreams mean's greatness and prominence. It means that you are destined for a prophetic and historic impact in the generation in which you live. Joseph dreamt about some of these symbols, and the interpretation he gave is no different from what I am sharing with you today. These installations are elements of prominence, in other words, God is showing you who you are and what will become of you in the immediate future, so that you can work towards it. Many people are confused in life; they don't know what really their

> **Interpretation**
>
> *The essence of stars, the moon, the sun and other installations in your dream means greatness and prominence.*

purpose is, that is one of the reasons why I believe the Holy Spirit leads us in numerous ways to fulfil our God given potentials. **Some times these symbols are revealed in your dreams as the sun, falling or the stars and the moon are falling, as if the world is coming to an end. When it happens that way, it simply means the coming of that great day of the Lord (the judgement day) .** This calls for a sober reflection and redemption of time, for the days are evil.

So you see, which ever way, the virtue of greatness articulated to these symbols cannot be over ruled.

Functional Prophetic Declaration:

Unto God who is able to keep me from falling and to present me blameless in my season, to Him who prepare my fingers for battle and my hands for war, to him that lifts up a standard against my enemies, and to Him that elevates me from the miry clay and sits me among princes, be the glory forever. He will guide my feet like a deer's feet and make me walk on my high places, Amen.

TOMATOES:- NOURISHMENT IN LIFE

Tomatos is one of the common symbols that can appear in one's dream. They are very significant to divine information and coded language. The meaning of tomatoes in your dream is nourishment to life. What I mean by nourishment to life is the enablement, the spring board to success, the drive, the favour and the capability of God's goodness in one's life.

Interpretation

The meaning of tomatoes in your dream is nourishment to life and prominence.

Symbolically, Tomatoes are elements of graceful blessing. When you sow them, harvest them, buy them, sell or cook with them in your dreams, God will cause your destiny to accelerate and grow into total abundance. Sometimes it can be a large tomato

Plantation which you may see yourself working in, or harvesting it. Other times too, it can be that, people have gathered a huge quantity and presented it to you as a gift. Which ever way you see it, it means you are nourished in the Grace of God. There are other symbols which have the same meaning or a similitude representation in your dreams; I will be sharing these with you in the next edition.

As far as your dreams are following such an impressive pattern, I see you overcoming swiftly to the other side of your destiny, keep moving forward!

Functional Prophetic Declaration:

Father you created me to make a difference, this is my season to shine, I thank you for the enablement and nourishment. By the power of your Holy Ghost I climb on the stairs of achievements and success limitlessly in the mighty name of Jesus, amen.

Scriptural Infusion
I will go before you and will level the mountains; I will break down gates of bronze and cut through bars of iron. I will give you the treasures of darkness, riches stored in secret places, so that you may know that I am the LORD, the God of Israel, who summons you by name. Isaiah 45:2-3.(NIV).

GRAIN / CEREALS:- BREAKTHROUGH AND PROSPERITY

Most of the symbols we are treating are common symbols we see in our everyday life. God chooses these common symbols, to fraternize with our comprehension. The devil also imitates this strategy. Cereals or grains mean a lot as far as dreams are concerned. Grains such as rice, maize, millet, wheat etc. symbolize and illustrate multiple ranges of blessings, breakthroughs, wealth, abundance and prosperity in every facet of your life, anytime you see them in your dreams. Large plantations or farms are connected to grains and cereals in your dreams. These dreams leads to prosperity in real life, many destinies have been transformed completely at the appearance of these most relevant symbols. Most Pastors have had their churches exploded into unspeakable numbers drastically, after certain divine visitations in their dreams.

Functional Prophetic Declaration:

I command God's commanded blessings to break forth expressly, streams of life to flow in a desert place, and way where there seems to be no way. As God is, so am I upon the earth. I am a true image and likeness of God. Nothing can change this in the name of Jesus.

Scriptural Infusion

May God give you of heaven's dew and of earth's richness an abundance of grain and new wine. May nations serve you and peoples bow down to you. Be

lord over your brothers, and may the sons of your mother bow down to you. May those who curse you be cursed and those who bless you be blessed."
Gen. 27:28-29.(NIV).

AIRPLANE:-
UPLIFTMENT

When you see yourself flying an airplane, or see yourself at the airport, or in a departure lounge, or anything to do with air travel, it means God's divine elevation or upliftment. The Holy Ghost will always make you knowledgeable of the magnitude of the progress allocated to you. Uncommon favours will characterize your destiny, any time you are airlifted in your dreams. Flying, loading your baggage into an aircraft or buying a ticket to fly an airplane,

Interpretation

Uncommon favours will characterize your destiny, any time you are airlifted in your dreams.

establishes a peculiar upliftment God is bringing your way.

Functional Prophetic Declaration:
Lord I thank you for remembering me, no matter what I am going through right now. I honour you for your divine intervention, my change has come the storm is over now. In Jesus name my enemies shall perish and be ashamed. Thank you, you have lifted up.

> **Scriptural Infusion**
> The LORD sends poverty and wealth; he humbles and he exalts. 1 Samuel 2:7.(NIV).

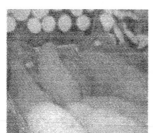

TUBERS:- FAVOUR / ABUNDANCE

A Tuber is basically a fleshly swollen underground stem. Crops which fall under such categories form an integral part of Human Existence. In real life, tubers provide enough food for human consumption. Some of these include: the various types of yam, cassava, potato etc. When you dream of working in such a plantation, or harvesting and selling any of these tubers, it means that, the favour and abundance of God will crown the dividends of whatsoever investments you have embarked upon. It also means that you will see multiplication in every facet of the works of your hands.

Interpretation

. *When you dream of working in such a plantation, or harvesting and selling any of these tubers, it means that, the favour and abundance of God will crown the dividends of whatsoever investments you have embarked upon.*

Functional Prophetic Declaration:

I speak multiplicity into every investment of my lifetime, I declare as the Lord lives I will see the fruit of my labour embedded in the favour of God. I will see clear manifestations of the fullness of the favour of God for the rest of my life in the mighty name of Jesus.

> **Scriptural Infusion**
> You will have plenty of goats' milk to feed your
> family and to nourish your women servants.
> Proverbs 27:27.(NIV).

WEARING BEAUTIFUL DRESSES:- HONOUR

For a person to be admired or seen to be beautiful, handsome or pleasant, one important factor that is mostly considered or observed is the person's physical appearance. This consists of make-up, apparel, fragrance, shoes and the type of colours the individual decorates or adorned him/herself with. In the same way, beautiful apparel in your dreams means honour. Dreaming of wearing torn or tattered clothes is degrading, and needs immediate prayer attention. Dreaming about torn and dirty clothes means depletion of one's destiny, shame and poverty. Beautiful apparels reflect the destiny of every dreamer, and determines his/her winning potential as well. The winning potential of a dreamer can also be linked to the specific colours of the apparel that are seen in their dreams. **Dreaming of nice and beautiful clothes also means unlimited Honou**r.

Interpretation

beautiful apparel in your dreams means honour. Dreaming of wearing torn or tattered clothes is degrading, and needs immediate prayer attention. Dreaming about torn and dirty clothes means depletion of one's destiny, shame and poverty.

Functional Prophetic Declaration:

Let the beauty of the Lord my God be upon me and establish the works of my hands, yes, and establish the works of my hands. Such shall be the potion of my children and my children's children to the third and forth generations to come. In Jesus name so shall it be established, so shall it be done!

Scriptural Infusion
Praise the LORD, my soul; all my inmost being,

> praise his holy name. Praise the LORD, my soul, and forget not all his benefits who forgives all your sins and heals all your diseases, who redeems your life from the pit and crowns you with love and compassion, who satisfies your desires with good things so that your youth is renewed like the eagle's. Psalm 103:1-5.(NIV).

LARGE PLANTATION/FARM:- COVENANT SUCCESS

Success is the trade mark for every spirit filled, tongue talking, bible believing and prudent child of God. Sometimes, you can dream, and see yourself in a very huge plantation covering vase acres of land. You cannot be financially deficient when you see dreams like that. It can only get better for you. Your father in Heaven's plan concerning you, is that of good and not of evil, to give you peace and success. Symbolically, when you own, work, till, harvest or walk through a large farm in your dream, it means that you are a success by the covenant blood of Jesus!

Interpretation

Symbolically, when you own, work, till, harvest or walk through a large farm in your dream, it means that you are a success by the covenant blood of Jesus!

Functional Prophetic Declaration:

The dew of heaven shall continually be mine, the fatness of the earth shall be mine, and plenty of corn shall locate me, so shall the fatness of the earth find me. By the grace of God, through me the families of the earth shall be blessed. They that bless me shall be blessed and they that curse me shall be cursed.

Scriptural Infusion

"I will make you into a great nation, and I will bless you; I will make your name great, and you will be a blessing. I will bless those who bless you, and whoever curses you I will curse; and all peoples on earth will be blessed through you." Gen. 12:2-3.(NIV)

AN ANOINTED MAN / WOMAN: - DIVINE VISITATION

Every child of God, or spirit filled Christian belongs to a particular local church, which is guided by a spiritual father who is the Head Pastor of that particular Church. An epiphany of a man or woman of God in your dream is spectacular and magnificent, because every real man or woman of God is a symbolic epiphany of the Holy Spirit in your dreams. When you encounter the ministration of a man or woman of God in your dreams, the totality of the Godhead has visited you for supernatural fortitude and rejuvenation.

Interpretation

When you encounter the ministration of a man or woman of God in your dreams, the totality of the Godhead has visited you for supernatural fortitude and rejuvenation.

Such dreams are very tangible and powerful to every modern day Christian. Irresistible, you will thrive, and increase in the anointing of the Holy Ghost when see anointed folks in your dreams. Your ministry will do well and your days will see the miraculous move of God. When all men say there is a casting down, you shall say there is a lifting up. Every visitation of God carries a strange virtue and power. And that is why you keep having dreams about men and women of the gospel of Jesus Christ.

Functional Prophetic Declaration:
The north wind shall bring me fresh breeze of renewal from the throne of God, the south wind shall blow refreshing waves of revival across my path, the east wind will maximize solitude for fortitude in my daily Christian life, and the west wind will infuse the balm of Gilead and the fragrant spices of Egypt into my prayer life for remarkable results in Jesus mighty name, amen!

Scriptural Infusion
Then Joseph said to his brothers, "I am about to die. But God will surely come to your aid and take you up out of

---

> this land to the land he promised on oath to Abraham, Isaac and Jacob."Gen. 50:24.(NIV).

OVER POWERING AN ENEMY: - DOMINION & VICTORY

Life as a matter of fact is full of battles, strife and contentions. These attributes of life sometimes recurs or appear in your dreams. Some consider it as ordinary and attach no importance to it. This has lead to the ruin and destruction of many legitimate destinies. The negligence of dreams, especially in which the dreamer is conquered by his /her opponent, is a major cause of destiny destruction, stagnancy and retardation of progress. When you fight and

Interpretation

When you fight and overpower an enemy or adversary in your dream, it means exceptional victory and dominion.

overpower an enemy or adversary in your dream, it means exceptional victory and dominion. Strife and contention in dreams can be frequent, but in most instances the born again, spirit filled anointed dreamer, will always receive supernatural energy from heaven to emerge triumphant. Anytime you struggle with faces known and unknown to you and overcome them, you climb the stairs of victory and dominion to perpetual rest.

Functional Prophetic Declaration:
Strengthen my muscles O God, rekindle the skill of my right hand, rejuvenate the source of my strength and let not my lamb run out of oil, neither let my head lack fresh oil. But let my shoes be iron and brass and as my days, so let my strength be. I will serve you for the rest of my life. Thank you Father for answered prayer, in Jesus name, amen.

> ### Scriptural Infusion
> The God of peace will soon crush Satan under your feet. The grace of our Lord Jesus be with you. Romans 16:20.(NIV).

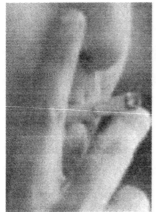

SMOKING IN YOUR DREAMS:- ILLUSTRATION OF THE ANOINTING

Many great men and women of God have encounted God and the power of His glory in diverse and meticulous ways. And also just by dreaming and seeing themselves smoking in their dreams. It is confusing isn't it? to hear that if you smoke in your dreams, it illustrates the anointing of the Holy Spirit. **Logic is not applicable when it comes to the supernatural!** The bible says he that is born of the spirit, is spirit, and he that is born of the flesh, is flesh. The spiritual person weighs all things spiritually. This is a mystery of God. You need the spirit of God to understand these mysteries. God symbolically reveals to the dreamer the essence and

Interpretation

if you smoke in your dreams, it illustrates the anointing of the Holy Spirit.

Significance of the unction in his or her life. During fasting and prayer if you discover in your dream that you are smoking, it is a clear indication of the release of the move of God into your spirit and your personal ministry.

Functional Prophetic Declaration:

Create in me a clean heart o Lord, and renew a right spirit within me. Cast me not away from your presence and take not your Holy Spirit from me, restore unto me the joy of your salvation and renew a right spirit within me, in the name of Jesus, amen.

Scriptural Infusion
And these are but the outer fringe of his works; how faint the whisper we hear of him! Who then can understand the thunder of his power?" Job 26:14.(NIV).

GOATS IN YOUR DREAM:- STUMBLING BLOCK

At anytime, if you dream of having any encounter whatsoever with goats in your dreams, it is the enemy's plan to hinder you from accomplishing and fulfilling your God-given potential, especially when embarking on a meaningful project or investment. You see, the devil has a prime agenda to steal, kill and destroy. This prime agenda of the devil is pursued with very diplomatic but crafty intelligence; it takes the spirit of God within you to read in between the lines. The devil is a lair! When you dream of goats chasing you, fighting you, following you, or talking to you, etc. it means a rebellious satanic revolt against your progress. It is a plan of the devil.

Interpretation
When you dream of Goats chasing you, fighting you, following you, or talking to you, etc. it means a rebellious satanic revolt against your progress. It is a plan of the devil.

Functional Prophetic Declaration:

No weapon formed against me shall prosper, and every tongue that rises against me in judgment I will condemn. This is my heritage in Christ Jesus and my righteousness is from Him who has delivered me from the domain of darkness and translated me into the kingdom of the living God. I know who I am! I am a child of God!

> ### Scriptural Infusion
> Yet I am always with you; you hold me by my right hand. You guide me with your counsel, and afterward you will take me into glory. Whom have I in heaven but you? And earth has nothing I desire besides you.
> Psalm 73: 23,24-25.(NIV).

FIGHTING IN DREAM: - EVIL CONTENTION

W hen a dreamer begin to fight known and unknown faces in their dreams it means the devil has opened a field to antagonize your blessing. This calls for a radical fight back through prayer. Most people who have had dreams like that will testify that the Holy Ghost intervenes by giving you strength to overcome the enemy in the dream. Married couples usually encounter dreams of this nature.

This is the devils plan to destabilize the marriage fidelity and cause divorce, but the devil is a liar! People normally dream of fighting with their mothers, fathers, brothers, sisters and sometimes even their spouse and children.

Interpretation

When a dreamer begins to fight known and unknown faces in their dreams it means the devil has opened a field to antagonize your blessing.

Whiles waiting for a favourable response from your employer, bankers, home office, etc. Don't entertain such antagonistic dreams; deal with it, in Jesus Name.

Functional Prophetic Declaration:
The battle is not mine; the battle is the Lord's. I will stand still and see the salvation of the Lord who prepares my fingers for battle and my hands for war. For He that is in me is greater than he that is in the world in Jesus mighty name I am more than a conqueror and more than a winner!

> **Scriptural Infusion**
> Break the arms of the wicked and the evildoers;
> call them to account for their wickedness that
> would not otherwise be found out.
> Psalm 10:15.(NIV).

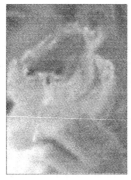

SHAVING YOUR HAIR:- DIMINISHED GLORY

In your dreams if you shave or barber your hair, or if you trim or cut your hair it means the favour or glory or the beauty of God upon your destiny, is marked for satanic demolishing and diminishing. The token or the symbol of your hair in your visions or dreams means the favour and special Grace God has bestowed upon you. If you see known or unknown faces attempting or in the process of shaving your hair, it signifies that the devil is in the process of erasing the magnitude of glory and honour placed on your life. The enemy targets masculinity (men) and femininity (women) respectively, with diabolic interference and resistance.

Revoke such dreams immediately and stand for your

Interpretation

In your dreams if you shave or barber your hair, or if you trim or cut your, it means the favour or glory or the beauty of God upon your destiny, is marked for satanic demonishing and diminiship kingdom right, because you have the life of God in you. Take Charge!

Functional Prophetic Declaration:

A thousand shall fall at my side and a ten thousand shall fall at my right hand, but it shall not come near me, with only my eyes will I behold the total destruction of the enemy. I declare prophetically that every arrow of the enemy shall fail; I am untouchable and indisputable in Jesus mighty name.

Scriptural Infusion

When the wicked advance against me to devour me, it is my enemies and my foes who will stumble and fall.
Psalm 27:2 (NIV).

SEX IN DREAMS:-
SPIRITUAL BONDAGE

Social commentators call sexual intercourse in dreams 'wet dreams' that is the lie of the devil! If you have been having sex in your dreams, you are spiritually bond and you are enslaved to Evil spiritual forces that will crush your destiny unless by God's Divine intervention. The following are the evil forces that enslave you when you keep having sexual intercourse in your dreams:

a) The spirit of Debts:- attacks your finances.

b) The spirit of Luke warmness:- destabilizes Christian life (Your prayer life begins to grow cold).

c) The spirit of infirmity:- attacks your body with satanic sicknesses or diseases which normally cannot respond to medical therapy, because they are spiritually transferred through dreams to affect your physical body.

d) The spirit of barrenness:- attacks your fertility potential and conception becomes imperative except with God's supernatural intervention.

e) The spirit of singleness:- incapacitate your power to get married. Many single people are frustrated because their marriages are delaying and they are growing old, especially the women.

f) The spirit of Depression:- takes your Joy away. And then you start feeling very down and very suicidal. I believe the numerous suicide stories our generation has recorded are the works of evil spirits.

g) The spirit of Obsession:- dominates and influences you not to be yourself. This spirit will control your will, mind, intellect and emotions. And that affects your decisions, choices and actions. Sex in dreams makes you a prisoner to satanic spirits.

h) Spirit of Lust:- attacks your dignity and integrity as a child of God. It deprives you from doing the right thing morally. Many great people have fallen into the traps of this deadly spirit.

i) Spirit of Possession:- This is where you become demon possessed. The devil came to steal, kill and to destroy. The final stage of the detriments of sexual dreams is for the devil to use your body as a vessel for evil, by possessing you.

Sex in dreams is dangerous, it is life threatening, It can strangle you to absolute distress. It is not subject to the principles of morals and decency, it can be between you and even mother, father, siblings, former boy/girl friend, husband, wife – these

Interpretation

If you have been having sex in your dreams, you are spiritually Bond and you are enslaved to Evil spiritual forces that will crush your destiny unless by God's Divine intervention.

are "familiar evil spirits". If it is with Animals, it is a curse, it means insinuations or a spell has been cast against you in the realm of the spirit.

Functional Prophetic Declaration:

I take dominion and authority now and reverse every deposits of the enemy in my life. I abort every conception of evil against me whatsoever; I declare a supernatural separation in the atmosphere or in the realm of the spirit at once. And I demand every ovation of evil to depart now, in the mighty name of Jesus, Amen.

Scriptural Infusion

I will not fear though tens of thousands assail me on every side. Arise, LORD!
Deliver me, my God! Strike all my enemies on the jaw; break the teeth of the wicked.
Psalm 3:7.(NIV).

INOCULATION IN DREAMS:- TRANSFERENCE OF SPIRITS

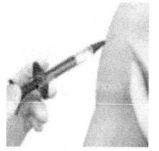

At anytime in your dreams, if you get injected or inoculated, it clearly means, the forces of infirmity and diseases have been released into your spirit to affect your body, that is why medicine and physicians cannot fathom 'certain sickness''. They are transferred in the spirit (through dreams most of the time). If care is not taken prayerfully with fasting, the dreamer's destiny will be incapacitated and impaired by such dreams.

I have seen many people suffer through this

Interpretation

At anytime in your dreams, if you get injected or inoculated, it clearly means, the forces of infirmity and diseases have been released into your spirit to affect your body, that is why medicine and physicians cannot fathom 'certain sickness''.

situation until Jesus made them free. When a demon possessed person in a family is about to die, and seeks to transfer the demon spirits to someone else in the family, he/she will do so through dreams among other means. That is why it's very important for parents or mentors to ask their children of the kind of dreams they dream at night and pay circumspective attention to what answers the children give. The devil operates in a realm where the persons involved are ignorant.

Functional Prophetic Declaration:

I resist and reject every possibility of transference of spirits. I come against every gathering of the devil; I diffuse and disperse it right now in Jesus name. Let every cultic and witchcraft powers be banish and flushed out of my life in the powerful name of Jesus! Not by my power not by my might, but by the Spirit of the Living God who lives in me.

Scriptural Infusion
"Do not allow a sorceress to live. Exodus 22:18.(NIV).

BABYSITTING IN YOUR DREAMS:- SET BACKS

When you babysit, Breast-feed children in your dreams, Nurse them or seeing children hung around you etc. Do not be deceived to think that it is a wonderful dream; Once a while, God will visit a barren woman who cannot give birth to children to encourage her that her prayers are not in vain, or God can describe the kind of child the dreamer is going to give birth to, the name of the child, the assignment of the child, the geographical location in which the child will be born into, the day, the time, etc and that dream will come to pass as the Lord has revealed it. But usually when you keep having dreams of feeding babies carrying them, it is a spiritual sabotage of the devil against

> ### Interpretation
> *when you keep having dreams of feeding babies carrying them, it is a spiritual sabotage of the devil against the dreamer's fertility potential.*

the dreamer's fertility potential. I have seen many whose lives have been going through circles without yielding any meaningful fruit. Sometimes, transference of spirits sets in, when you begin to have dreams like these, arise as a born again, spirit filled, tongue talking, bible believing, fire blazing, child of God and march out the demons! In Jesus Name!

Functional Prophetic Declaration:
I arrest every illegal trespassing operation of the devil in my life, and I reclaim and recover my supernatural properties instantly in Jesus name. I break the pattern of negative dreams from the tentacles of my future, and I resist any subsequent occurrence by the power of the Holy Ghost, amen!

Scriptural Infusion
Let death take my enemies by surprise; let them go down alive to the realm of the dead, for evil finds lodging among them.
Psalm 52:15 (N.I.V).

CRABS:- DISASTER AND TROUBLE.

The Devil normally targets everything that brings comfort and joy to the dreamer, and intercept's it with terrible dreams which are symbolized by crabs. Sometimes it is black crabs other times too it is red crabs. The devil's intention is to disrupt you and shift you from God. Crabs represent terrible trouble and disaster in your dreams and visions, whether they are red or black. **God reveals to redeem!** The moment a dreamer begins to dream about crabs, there is some pre-calculated evil agenda of the devil to flush you out. Determine through fervent Prayer that every conception of terrible news shall be aborted and disintegrated pre-mutually by

Interpretation

The devil's intention is to disrupt you and shift you from God. Crabs represent terrible trouble and disaster in your dreams and visions, the powers of the scriptures in Jesus mighty name!

Functional Prophetic Declaration:

I announce to the universe and to the spirit world, that there is no storm discovered under the sun that can be able to antagonize and overpower me. I am irrefutably fortified like a flint of rock. I rebel against every pre-calculated demonic agenda of the enemy; I declare the perpetual rest of the Holy Ghost to compass my life in Jesus name!

Scriptural Infusion
They triumphed over him by the blood of the Lamb and by the word of their testimony; they did not love their lives so much as to shrink from death.
Revelation 12:11. (NIV).

NAKED IN DREAMS:- LACK OF FAVOUR

Most people wonder what it means to be naked in your dreams. It is a mystery! When you walk naked, or half naked, or someone striping you naked, or anything associated with nakedness in your dreams; or sometimes trying to cover your nakedness; also when people watch your nakedness especially the opposite sex and laugh at you, it means, disgrace, shame, setbacks, financial barrenness, a circle of disappointment and defeat.

Dreamers who normally have these

Interpretation

When you walk naked, or half naked, or someone striping you naked, or anything associated with nakedness in your dreams; or sometimes trying to cover your nakedness; also when people watch your nakedness especially the opposite sex and laugh at you, means, disgrace, shame, setbacks, financial barrenness, a circle of disappointment and defeat.

dreams hardly see success and progress. They mostly complain that they cannot succeed in anything they do. The devil by these dreams depletes your legitimate destiny and steals the favour that has been bestowed on you by God. Some dreamers say everything will be moving smoothly until suddenly when such dreams start. My Darling, Do not wait until you loose everything before you begin to beg for what belongs to you, fight back, and repossess what is yours!

Functional Prophetic Declaration:

I will not be disgraced; neither will I be ashamed, as the Lord lives and my soul remains before His throne I will triumph beyond every trap and entanglement of the devil. Devil, I want you to know that you are fighting a losing battle! You can never win against me, I am the battle axe of the Lord, sharper and tenacious, and I will never give-up in Jesus name!

Scriptural Infusion

But the LORD is righteous; he has cut me free from the cords of the wicked." May all who hate Zion be turned

back in shame."
Psalm 129:4-5 (NIV).

LOST IN DREAMS:-
STAGNATION

Most dreamers' progression has been haltered through their dreams by this spirit of stagnancy. If you dream and cannot make your way through, or you find yourself in a strange land and you realize you are lost or stranded, it basically means you are stagnant in life. Being static in life can be a result of this calibre of dreams. It has crippled giants and icons, refuse to be a victim.

Interpretation

. If you dream and cannot make your way through, or you find yourself in a strange land and you realize you are lost or stranded, it basically means you are stagnant in life.

Subsequently, if you join a bus, train, plane or car and whiles in motion, the journey is never reaching its destination, or the driver is lost, it also means stagnation. Refuse to be controlled, start controlling your world! You are the righteousness of God in Christ Jesus!

Functional Prophetic Declaration:

I refuse, I reject, I abort, I terminate, and I disintegrate and disengage every static and stagnant trend of my life. I regain my God given inheritance and progression in this life. I capture all the years eaten by the locust and the caterpillar in Jesus name.

Scriptural Infusion
"The wicked earn deceptive wages, but those who sow righteousness reap a sure reward."
Proverbs 11:18 (NIV).

DEAD PEOPLE IN YOUR DREAMS:- FAMILIAR SPIRITS

The devil is crafty; he came to steal, kill and to destroy. He does so through deceptive and manipulative means. For instance, if you meet a horrifying and unknown creature in your dreams, I don't think you will give it any meaningful attention, but if you meet your dead relatives in your dreams you will, Why? Because you loved them before they died.

In other words the devil uses the facial appearance of your dead relatives to put his agenda across, that's why we call such evil spirits "familiar spirits". In your

Interpretation

In your dreams, if you see people who are dead come and communicate with you, give you gifts or take things from you, or even invite you to join them in the place where they are; it is not of the lord, it is the work of the devil!

dreams, if you see people who are dead come and communicate with you, give you gifts or take things from you, or even invite you to join them in the place where they are; it is not of the lord, it is the work of the devil!

Nevertheless, **once in a hundred God can use the facial Appearance of a dead relative to pass a divine information on to you.** I repeat once in a hundred!

Dust has returned to dust, and ashes has departed to ashes, and bible says the spirit of man has returned back to his God!

Functional Prophetic Declaration:
There is no temptation taken me but such as is common to man, but God is faithful, who will not suffer me to be tempted above that which I am able; but will with the temptation also make a way of escape, that I will be able to bear it!

Scriptural Infusion
Moses answered the people, "Do not be afraid. Stand firm and you will see the deliverance the LORD will

---

bring you today. The Egyptians you see today you will never see again. The LORD will fight for you; you need only to be still."
Exodus 14:13-14 (NIV)

GUN SHOT:- SIGN OF DEATH

There is a lady I know who had a dream and was shot in her bedroom by a gunman. The next morning she woke-up to discover a bullet physically next to her bed. Three days after she collapsed in that same bedroom and was taken to the hospital. She remained in the hospital for three months till she regained consciousness. One Saturday afternoon whiles listening to my radio program she phoned-in to

Interpretation

When you hear the sound of a gun in your dream, or when you see someone pointing a gun at you to shoot you, or someone else, it is a sign of death against you the dreamer or a close relative. Massive explosives, grenades, etc are all signs of death.

testify how the devil attacked her with a gunshot in her dream, and how Jehovah God delivered her miraculously.

When you hear the sound of a gun in your dream, or when you see someone pointing a gun at you to shoot you, or someone else, it is a sign of death against you the dreamer or a close relative.

Massive explosives, grenades, etc are all signs of death. My question is, why do you allow Satan to terminate your life prematurely? Free Yourself!

Functional Prophetic Declaration:
I am troubled on every side, yet not distressed. Perplexed, but not in despair. Persecuted, but not forsaken. Cast down but not destroyed. For my light affliction which is but for a moment works for me a far more exceeding and eternal weight of glory in Jesus name!

Scriptural infusion
Appoint someone evil to oppose my enemy; let an accuser stand at his right hand. When he is tried, let him be found guilty, and may his prayers condemn him.

May his days be few; may another take his place of leadership. May his children be fatherless and his wife a widow. May his children be wandering beggars; may they be driven from their ruined homes. May a creditor seize all he has; may strangers plunder the fruits of his labor. May no one extend kindness to him or take pity on his fatherless children. May his descendants be cut off, their names blotted out from the next generation.

Psalm 109:6-13.(NIV)

CHARCOAL:- SIGN OF DEATH

Charcoal is an emphatic symbol of death to every dreamer. Once in a hundred, the spirit of God can use this symbol to depict the anointing of the Holy Spirit. **Selling, buying, being given or cooking with charcoal is a clear indication of death against a close relative or a loved one.** Peradventure, if a family begins to loose its

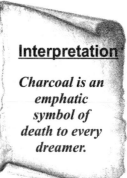

Interpretation

Charcoal is an emphatic symbol of death to every dreamer.

members to death continuously and unusually, in real sense, any member of the family who dreams of charcoal has seen a revelation of demonic premature and untimely deaths. Investment of prayer must be mixed with intense fasting for your loved ones when you have such dreams, to deliver them from pre-mature death in Jesus Name! Normally when dreamers begin to have such dreams they panic and begin to accommodate fear, timidity and anxiety.

That is when the devil gain grounds and continue to entrench his evil schemes on you. Stump that fear out! And take charge in Christ today!

Functional Prophetic Declaration:

As for me and my house we will not die, but we shall live and declare the works of God. For who is he that says and it comes to pass when God has not ordered it? We are the workmanship of God created in His true image and likeness, to make a difference in this life and the one to come, Amen!

Scriptural infusion
This day the LORD will deliver you into my hands, and

I'll strike you down and cut off your head. This very day I will give the carcasses of the Philistine army to the birds and the wild animals, and the whole world will know that there is a God in Israel.
1 Samuel 17:46. (NIV).

COFFINS IN Y OUR DREAM:- SIGN OF DEATH

Vividly, many people have been dreaming of caskets or coffins at diverse times. Most of these people are Christians who love the Lord, go to church, and pay their tithes and live right. If you have been dreaming of coffins, sometimes it is God who is revealing to you the ulterior motives or hidden agenda of the devil and to redeem you from it. Other times it is the

Interpretation

If you have been dreaming of coffins, sometimes it is God who is revealing to you the ulterior motives or hidden agendas of the devil and to redeem you from it.

adversary the devil who wants to impose his perverse incantations on you. But whatever the situation coffins or caskets symbolizes death channelled against you the dreamer or a close relative.

When a dreamer begins to see coffins and funeral services and gathering, or see obituaries of known and unknown faces; extra attention must be given to prayer and fasting.

If you've had any similitude or a prototype of the above mentioned dreams the standard of the Holy Ghost must be lifted against the forces of darkness at once, for you are seated in Christ far above principalities and Powers!

Functional Prophetic Declaration:
I shall not die before my time, and I will not be assassinated by any evil force whatsoever in the heaven above or in the earth beneath. I refuse every iota of untimely death, and cast it into the pit of hell, and overrule every advances of mischief perpetrated in dark places in Jesus name!

Scriptural infusion

After I looked things over, I stood up and said to the nobles, the officials and the rest of the people, "Don't be afraid of them. Remember the Lord, who is great and awe-some, and fight for your people, your sons and your daughters, your wives and your homes." When our enemies heard that we were aware of their plot and that God had frustrated it, we all returned to the wall, each to our own work.
Nehemiah 4:14-15. (NIV).

Interpretation

Mourning cloths signifies death.

MOURNING CLOTHES:- SIGN OF DEATH

The most pathetic and deadly commodity in life is ignorance. The apostle Paul wrote. "I do not want you to be ignorant of the devices of Satan. Many people ignorantly call some of these devices "superstitions". Mourning cloths signifies death. If you see people mourning, wailing, or crying in your dreams, it means that the spirit of death is hunting for the life of somebody dear to your heart.

The mourning clothes universally are Black and Red. I will be sharing insightfully with you the essence of colours in your dreams in the volume two of this book. Untimely death is an orchestration of Satan, it is not of God, and it mostly begins in your dreams.

Many a time we take such dreams for granted and make comments like 'it was just a dream,' no my darling, it was not just a dream. It is Satan's snare to kill you. Rise and stop him now by the power of Jehovah!

Functional Prophetic Declaration:
I saturate the atmosphere with the power of the Holy Ghost, and I nullify the realm of my world with the undefiled blood of Jesus. The fear of death is hereby prohibited indefinitely by the command of my voice, at the mention of the name Jesus, Son of the Most High God, Amen !

Scriptural infusion

"Truly I tell you, whatever you bind on earth will be bound in heaven, and whatever you loose on earth will be loosed in heaven.
Matthew 18:18. (NIV).

DEEP PIT & DITCH: - SIGN OF DEATH

One Saturday afternoon whiles conducting my radio program, an intelligent young lady called into the program and said she had a dream that she was holding three tubers of yam and she was going to plant them in a field. When she got to the field, she discovered a very deep pit in front of her, she panicked and went back, whiles she was stepping back, she stumbled and one of the tubers of yam fell into the deep pit, while contemplating on how to get it out, she woke up. By the grace of God through revelation knowledge, this is the interpretation the Holy

Spirit gave me for her;

The three tubers of yams are three children, the field means the world or life, and the deep pit means death. As soon as I finished talking the lady began to cry on the telephone. With curiosity I ascertain from her what the problem was, and she remarked painfully that she is a single mother of three girls and just 3 weeks after the dream she lost her second girl.

She exclaimed, because she did not understand the dream she brushed if off. Also she was shocked at the interpretation and its occurrence. The meaning of deep pits or ditches in your dreams mean death against the dreamer or a close relative or loved one.

Functional Prophetic Declaration:
Every mountain shall become like a flat plain and every valley shall be exalted before me. I speak life and life abundantly into the lives of everyone connected to my destiny. I divert all my love ones from the brim of death, and I seek refuge in the secret place of the most high, we shall abide under

the shadow of the almighty in Jesus name!

Scriptural infusion
You will not fear the terror of night, nor the arrow that flies by day, nor the pestilence that stalks in the darkness, nor the plague that destroys at midday. A thousand may fall at your side, ten thousand at your right hand, but it will not come near you. You will only observe with your eyes and see the punishment of the wicked. If you say, "The LORD is my refuge," and you make the Most High your dwelling, no harm will overtake you, no disaster will come near your tent. For he will command his angels concerning you to guard you in all your ways; Psalm 91:5-11.(NIV).

SEEING YOURSELF DEAD IN YOUR DREAMS:- SIGN OF DEATH

Interpretation
But the main point here is when you see yourself dead. The meaning is death against you the dreamer or a loved one.

T here is a strange delicacy that happens in

the "dream world", to see your self performing an act but at the same time you see yourself standing aside beholding your self performing the act. For example, in your dream if you see yourself playing football and at the same time you are watching on as a spectator, amazing isn't it? That's dreams for you!

But the main point here is when you see yourself dead. The meaning is death against you the dreamer or a loved one. Many people have shared with me the experience of seeing themselves standing and beholding themselves laid in state or being put in the mortuary, or even being buried. The mystery in this phenomenon is the separation of the spirit from the soul, anytime you see yourself "twice or dual" in your dream it's a display and illustration of your spirit away from your soul. And this is a sign of death against you the dreamer. It is a signal of untimely death. Resist the devil and he will flee from you!

Functional Prophetic Declaration:
When the enemy comes in like a flood against me, the Spirit of God will lift up a standard against

him. For the Lord is with me as a strong and terrible one, therefore all my persecutors will stumble, they shall not prevail, they shall be greatly ashamed, for they shall not prosper, their everlasting confusion shall be forgotten in the name of Jesus the Christ!

Scriptural infusion

Mightier than the thunder of the great waters, mightier than the breakers of the sea — the LORD on high is mighty.   Psalm 93:4. (NIV).

COINS IN YOUR DREAMS:- TOTAL POVERTY

Even though coins are legal tender used for viable transaction in real life, I will have to reiterate that what is spirit is spirit, and what is flesh is flesh. Spiritual things are spiritually discerned and physical things are also physically assessed. But when it comes to the subject of dreams you cannot mix or induce physical logic to supernatural apocalypse. It takes the spirit of God and the anointing to accurately interpret a dream, vision, prophecy, etc. just like Daniel and Joseph did.

Coins in your dreams are symbols of barrenness, poverty, insufficiency, curses, disappointments, marginalization, and regression.

Interpretation

Coins in your dreams are symbols of barrenness, poverty, insufficiency, curses, disappointments, marginalization, and regression.

Coins in your dreams are symbols of barrenness, poverty, insufficiency, curses, disappointments, marginalization, and regression. When you make a transaction with coins in your dreams it means poverty, when you cash or you are being given coins, or collecting them whatsoever, it all means financial barrenness and bankruptcy! When you change your note currency into coins it means absolute poverty, scarcity and indebtedness. The Urgency of prayer is crucial to any person who might have had a prototype or such kind of dreams. Such dreams have crippled many businesses, marriages, churches and their pastors, governments and nations!

Functional Prophetic Declaration:

God, let elements that fight my progress be disarmed, when they advance against me to devour my flesh, let them stumble and fall. If they encamp against me, frustrate their efforts, If they launch their attacks, let it not be of you, and if they monitor my steps, let them turn back in the mighty name of Jesus

Scriptural infusion

The wicked band together against the Righteous and condemn the innocent to death. But the LORD has become my fortress, and my God the rock in whom I take refuge. He will repay them for their sins and destroy them for their wickedness; the LORD our God will destroy them.
Psalm 94:21-23. (NIV).

HUMAN WASTE (TOILET) IN YOUR DREAMS:- RETROGRESSION AND POVERTY

Many people have been deceived to believe that if you have any encounter with human execrator it is wealth, what a lie of the devil! I shared with you in the previous pages that supernatural illumination cannot be understood with a logical mentality. Toilet, human excreta or faeces is one of the deadly symbols the enemy uses to destroy the dreamers future. By revelation knowledge I have learnt that every person who keeps having such dreams keeps sinking in life except by the supernatural intervention of

Interpretation
The meanings of human waste/toilet in your dreams are retrogression, setbacks, confusion, disaster, calamity, shame, disgrace, frustration and total poverty.

God.

The meanings of human waste/toilet in your dreams are retrogression, setbacks, confusion, disaster, calamity, shame, disgrace, frustration and total poverty. When dreams of human waste persist, retrogression and poverty may encapsulate the dreamer's world. That is why I believe that God has given me this ministerial and revelational gift to bring accurate precision to great people like you.

Many men and women have become financially bankrupt and ineffective because even though they keep having these dreams, they lack the new creation attitude and faith to make a difference!

Prayer can stop it! The word of God can stop it! Your faith In Christ can stop it! The anointing of the Holy Ghost upon your life can also stop it! Stop it today!

Functional Prophetic Declaration:
The blessings of the Lord makes rich and adds no sorrow to it. My portion of wealth allocated to me

in the land of the living cannot be reallocated, for the gifts of God are without repentance. I cease my divine opportunity and make maximum utilization of it. I grab what is mine and I refuse to let go, in Jesus mighty name!

> **Scriptural infusion**
> Fire goes before him and consumes his foes on every side.
> Psalm 97:3. (NIV).

REFUSE DAMP IN YOUR DREAM: - CONFUSION AND ANARCHY

It is fascinating, looking at how dignified you are, to dream and see yourself standing or walking on a refuse dump or rubbish site in your dreams. It leaves you with a lot of laudable questions and contemplations when you get up in the morning to realize it was a dream. The first of the numerous questions that comes to you is what is the meaning of this? It is the plan of Satan to counter-react and twist your speed and drive in life. The clear meanings of a refuse site or refuse dump in your dreams are chaos, anarchy, confusion, satanic conspiracy and mental or postnatal depression.

Interpretation
The clear meanings of a refuse site or refuse dump in your dreams are chaos, anarchy, confusion, satanic conspiracy and mental or postnatal depression.

Marriage Couples, nursing mothers, leaders or people of repute positions of co-operate entities, and young people preparing for marriage can sometimes dream of standing or having something to do at a refuse site.

The mischief of Satan is to derail you from your course, but the devil is already defeated. I know so many single people who were preparing to get married and after one of them (the man or the woman) dreaming walking, standing, sitting or sleeping on a refuse dump; destroyed their relationships.

I also know people who were waiting for a favourable reply from the home office but had a bitter experience after encountering dreams at the refuse dump. Wage war on the kingdom of darkness today and heaven will back you to victory and total triumph.

Functional Prophetic Declaration:
According to the word of the Lord, I force the devil to pay me back in a sevenfold of every blessing he tempered with in my life. The battle lines are drawn, and the host of heaven and even God is on my side. I am a stranger to failure; I will serve my generation with distinction and finish my course well in Jesus name, amen!

Scriptural infusion
When the wicked advance against me to devour me, it is my enemies and my foes who will stumble and fall. Though an army besiege me, my heart will not fear; though war break out against me, even then I will be confident.   Psalm 27:2-3. (NIV).

REPTILES IN YOUR DREAMS:- DEMONS

In most of the convention meetings we've hosted by the grace of God, from Accra to some of the cities around the world, I have discovered an intriguing scenario of adults who scream at night, only to wake-up to say that I had a very terrible nightmare.

What people call "nightmares" are all encounters with demons, that is one of the reason why they scream before they get up. If you have children who keep yelling in the night I believe that they need prayer and deliverance!

As for adults who occasionally scream in the night, with fear in their hearts and sweat all over their body; it is not only serious, but also ridiculous! If

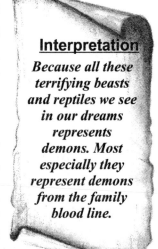

Interpretation
Because all these terrifying beasts and reptiles we see in our dreams represents demons. Most especially they represent demons from the family blood line.

you are a Christian and you keep having such dreams check your Christian life critically. Because all these terrifying beasts and reptiles we see in our dreams represents demons. Most especially they represent demons from the family blood line.

Lizards, crocodiles, snakes, alligators, etc are all creeping animals or reptiles. All such animals symbolically represent demons from ones family blood line. When you see them fighting with, chasing you, attacking you, intimidating you etc. shake off the dust of lukewarmness and fight back prayerfully.

Enforce your birthright as a child of God and set yourself loose. Normally such dreams are to cripple your success but your help is in the name of the lord.

Functional Prophetic Declaration:
There is no demon from the bottomless pit who can invade my life and take away my treasure, I intercept quickly and hastily and change the story in the mighty name of Jesus! Devil, I want you to

know that I am not afraid of you, neither am I ignorant of your devises, I stump you out NOW!

Scriptural infusion

I know that my redeemer lives, and that in the end he will stand on the earth.
Job 19:25. (NIV).

TORN CLOTHS IN YOUR DREAMS:- DEMOTION AND DEFEAT

One of the dangers in this life is to dream of seeing yourself and other people wearing torn, tatted or dirty clothes. When you wear wretched, dirty, tattered and torn clothes in your dreams it means financial setbacks, regression, defeat and shame of your destiny. See, your clothes illustrates your image, impact, influence or your personality. If you dream of wearing cloths of the above mentioned fashion, it is to demote you from where the Lord has set for you to where Satan wishes to place you.

Refuse that exchange! Reclaim what belongs to you! In your dreams if you see other people wearing your clothes, it means the exchange of your heritage and destiny for something worthless. Satan is exchanging what God gave you to pour into other people's lives. Take your place!

Interpretation
When you wear wretched, dirty, tattered and torn clothes in your dreams it means financial set backs, regression, defeat and shame of your destiny

Functional Prophetic Declaration:

I have overcome the devil by the blood of the Lamb and by the word of my testimony. No matter what the enemy does I am more than a conqueror seated in Christ very high above every principality, powers, and thrones and rulers of darkness in Jesus name!

Scriptural infusion

You made my enemies turn their backs in flight, and I destroyed my foes. They cried for help, but there was no one to save them — to the LORD, but he did not answer. I beat them as fine as windblown dust; I trampled them by like mud in the streets.
Psalm 18:40-42.(NIV).

BEING CHASED IN YOUR DREAMS:- SPIRITUAL OPPOSITION

In God's infinite wisdom He created sleep as an art of rest that after a long period of labour you will retreat and rest. So every human person goes to bed to sleep and get some rest, it is nourishment and health to your body. But so many people get up in the morning feeling very tired and weak as if they've been working whole night to the extent that most people wake-up in the morning feeling very exhausted, having migraine headache's as a result of fighting in their dreams or being chased by all manner of forces.

Interpretation

The meaning of being chased in your dreams is spiritual opposition, resistance, controversy, battle, satanic hindrances, blockades, contention and demonic barriers.

Sometimes in your dreams when these "forces" start to chase you, you begin to run, but whiles running you are not in motion (moving your legs but not making any forward advancement). Sometimes you feel some force is pressing you down and in the process you want to shout the name of Jesus but you cannot. The meaning of being chased in your dreams is spiritual opposition, resistance, controversy, satanic hindrances, blockades, and demonic barriers.

You must be determine and wake up to serious prayer when you are being chased in your dreams by a mad person, cows, lions, dogs, cats and wild creatures. Don't be ignorant from today! Such dreams tell's you there is some magnitude of hindrance or resistance to your progression and success. Diffuse all similar dreams with the blood of Jesus in Jesus name and disengage your life from spiritual opposition.

Stop asking why me? And start fighting the good fight of faith. The devil is trying to resist you because you are a solution to somebody's problem and because you interceded for someone or made a difference in the life of somebody.

Functional Prophetic Declaration:

I summon all such dreams to the throne of God for eternal justice. I subdue, deflate and superimpose the council of God over every manipulation of the enemy. My God is love, and love covers a multitude of sins, therefore love will overshadow every component of evil, for his banner over me is love!

Scriptural infusion

The LORD is my shepherd, I lack nothing. He makes me lie down in green pastures, he refreshes my soul. He guides me along the right paths for his name's sake. Even though I walk through the darkest valley, I will fear no evil, for you are with me; your rod and your staff, they comfort me. You prepare a table before me in the presence of my enemies. You anoint my head with oil; my cup overflows. Surely your goodness and love will follow me all the days of my life, and I will dwell in the house of the LORD forever.
Psalm 23. (NIV).

PRAYER TRANSFUSION

Nothing happens unless we pray and act on our holy faith. When it comes to the subject of prayer in connection with dreams, you cannot just be sounding words into the atmosphere, but to have the willingness, readiness, desire, love, and heart for viable prayers. Your connectivity or subscription to the help and intervention of Almighty God is based on the intensity of your prayer life.

Praise and worship is a very powerful weapon. When our praises goes up the glory of God comes down, when our worship ascend the highest altitude in the presence of God His blessings comes down into every situation that faces us. But prayer is the greatest weapon of every child of God. The effectiveness of the prayer of a sanctified born again believer is such amazing, it does not even matter what the problem is; they will give way to the will of God concerning your life by the power of prayer. Many people underestimate the potential and

Many people under-estimate the potential and need of a personal prayer life.

need of a personal prayer life.

I believe in praying with people, standing by them side by side in prayer with one accord, but I also believe in helping people to pray on their own. If you depend solely on your pastor or prophet to always pray for you, you will be totally disappointed in the day of trouble. Develop your personal prayer life today to the pinnacle where God wants it to be.

Be careful for nothing, but in everything by prayer and supplication with thanksgiving let your requests be made known unto God.   Philippians 4:6

So many Dreamers' complain of praying about their dreams and yet they keep having horrible dreams. Let me quickly say that every door has its own keys; you cannot use the wrong keys for the right door. Therefore the application of principles based on God's word is inevitable when it comes to praying concerning your dreams.

If you keep having weird dreams and you don't give it a prayerful attention it is very likely for the devil to capitalize upon your "prayerlessness" and fight against your destiny. Most of the disaster's that surround some Christians could be easily avoided by the investment of quality prayer. The easiest way to pray, is to pray!

The easiest way to pray, is to pray!

The effectual fervent prayer of the righteous man availeth much. James 5:6

As a dreamer you must always possess some magnitude or measure of prayer in your spirit at all times, that alone is a deterrent force against bad dreams.

As a dreamer you must always possess some magnitude or measure of prayer in your spirit at all times, that alone is a deterrent force against bad dreams.

Make a deliberate and an intentional decision to stop the enemy from destroying your God given destiny, it is possible! Begin with faith, then with discipline, then consistency, then tenacity, then with a positive winning attitude, then with the word of God, then with prophetic confessions and lastly with the anointing of the Holy Ghost. Pray in tongues if you have that gift, if not pray with your understanding, but do pray. The devil is afraid of praying men and women; he cannot stand the flames of spirit filled prayer.

But dear beloved, building up yourself in your most Holy Faith, and praying in the Holy Ghost. Jude 1:20

One secret of praying about your dreams is, whether you understand the dream or not, PRAY!

Don't wait for the interpretation of a dream before you pray. Maintain a lifestyle of prayer, and pray about your dream life daily it is very crucial to your success.

Disengagement prayer

Disengagement prayer is the power to defuse, disperse or separate satanic conspiracies from your destiny by the powers of the scriptures. To disengage is to course a massive separation of two entities. I believe it is time for certain things and events to Part Company with you forever.

This kind of prayer is a very radical type of prayer that leaves the devil with no choice than to advice himself and back-off!

Praying always with all prayers and supplication in the spirit and watching thereunto with all perseverance and supplication for all saints. Ephesians 6:18.

This kind of prayer is a very radical type of prayer that leaves the devil with no choice than to advice himself and back-off!

The praying of disengagement prayers requires the leading of a holy and a sanctified life, because such warfare with the enemy is a crucial one. Optimistically, it is appropriate, to position yourself spiritually, morally, and psychologically on the winning side.

6 STEPS TO DISENGAGEMENT PRAYER

1.   Pray with a sound mind.

A lot of people pray with their attention on something else, and because the prayer lacks concentration it becomes unfruitful. Many people pray for hours with virtually zero sound mind.

A sound mind is an attribute of God; He has not given us the spirit of fear but power, love and a sound mind. Praying with a sound mind is extremely important, as a matter of fact, disengaging negative dreams needs a sound mind in addition to other appropriate virtues to be effective and triumphant.

> A sound mind is an attribute of God;

2.   Pray Prophetically.

Declare God's prophetic agenda concerning your

life as you pray. Pronounce statements like 'as the Lord lives and my soul lives, not a hair of my head will fall to the ground, for I am an earth blesser, ordained by God in eternity before time to reign upon the earth'. The devil is terrified by Christians who know their rights and privileges.

3. Pray by the powers of the Scriptures.

The word was with God from the beginning; all things were made by the word, and without the word was not anything made that was made. In the word is life and this life is the light of men. Scripture is the word of God! And the word of God is sharper than any two edge sword. Memorize the scriptures and quote them when you are praying, especially when you are praying about your dreams. In the city of Ephesus, so mightily grew the word of God and prevailed! The word of God will prevail in your life and shall not fail!

4. Pray Fervently.

The devil cannot resist the effectual fervent

prayer of the righteous, such prayers are very powerful. It doesn't mean anything if all you can do is to pray boring and non-effective prayers; it's just a waste of time. Some negative dreams are so tangible and real that it provokes you to a radical action. Cultivate the attitude of fervent prayers and you will be glad you did.

He that speaks in an unknown tongue does not speak to man but speaks to God, for in the spirit he speaks mysteries. The devil cannot understand when you communicate to God in the language of the Holy Ghost, it can only be understood by God and them that have the mind of Christ, and therefore praying in tongues edifies you. It doesn't mean that when you don't pray in tongues you are not in the spirit, praying in the spirit is the work of the Holy Ghost, even when you pray with your understanding by the power of the Holy Ghost it is spiritually and equally powerful!

6.   Pray with Authority.
Take dominion and enforce divine law. It is pathetic that so many Christians don't know who

they are in Christ; they have a major identity crisis! It is just like having a loaded weapon in your possession and crying for help at the attack of an importer, ridiculous! Pray with authority and power, release the unction in y o u a n d silence the devil.

DISENGAGING NEGATIVE DREAMS

1. Be quick to pray. Waste no time, procrastinate no more and wake up to reality. The word of God says "when men slept after they have sown good seeds, an enemy came and sowed tares among the good seeds". Tares is the work of the devil, it can only be sown when men sleep, when they become weak and vulnerable, but you do not belong to the fragile company of backsliding folks, but to the militant battalion of God's end time generals.

2. **Refuse the dream in your mind or in your spirit.**
Delete every evil dream by the power of the Holy

Ghost "out-rightly" out of your system. A bad dream becomes a stigma on you when you ignorantly accept it. The devil gains a foothold in an atmosphere of ignorance, and that is why the bible say's we are not ignorant of His devices. Reject his stuff with immediate effect!

3.   **Revoke a bad dream back to its source by the power of prayer.**

You have power invested in you by God to forgive and to retain sins, you also have power to bind and to loose, furthermore the power of life and   death is in your tongue, make use of it now! Redirect every satanic dream back to where it came from, and put the devil to where he belongs in the mighty name of Jesus!

4.   **Pray in the name of Jesus.**

There is no name given unto the sons of men in which they must be saved than the name of Jesus. At the mention of the name of Jesus, every knee shall bow and every tongue shall confess that Jesus is Lord to the glory of the   Father. The name of Jesus is powerful, it's an explosion, and it's a magnifying force and a compelling power. Call the name of Jesus and you shall be saved.

5.   Believe that it is done.

By faith the elders obtained a good report, the bible say's if we pray we must believe and we shall receive. Abraham staggered not at the promises of God through unbelief, but was strong in faith, giving God the glory; and being fully persuaded that, what God had promised, he was also able to perform. And therefore it was imputed to him for righteousness. Blessed are those who have not yet seen and yet they believe. Believe that all your prayers shall be answered, and it shall be done!

6.   Give thanks!

It is God who works in us both to will and to do His good pleasure. After Jesus had cleansed ten leapers, one of them turned back to give

Every prayer no matter what purpose must end with thanksgiving unto God for His love towards us.

thanks to Him. Every prayer no matter what purpose must end with thanksgiving unto God for His love towards us. If you pray against any negatively inclined dream conclude with appreciation unto God, who has not left you for your enemies to destroy you. He is good and His mercy endures forever, amen!

VALIDATING POSITIVE DREAMS.

1.   Write down your positive dream on a piece of paper and observe it as a daily prayer topic. It is very important to keep records of the dreams you dream at night, so that if they are positive dreams you can pray them through to manifestation, and also to give thanks to God for bringing his word to pass in your life or in other people's lives. If it is a negative dream it will remind you to pray against it without forgetting about it.

2.   Don't share your dreams with the wrong people; they do not have the heart for it. They

will envy you unnecessarily and kill your dream. Also do not let the wrong people try to interpret your dream; they will end up misleading you. When you misunderstand your dream, you misinterpret it and end up misapplying it.

Let the Holy Spirit of God lead you for the rest of your life.

3.   Pray for the manifestation of your positive dreams. I believe that God has a purpose for every dream that comes from His throne, you do not dream for fun, therefore discovering the real purpose of God concerning that particular dream is extremely inevitable. Ask God to show you His glory in this time of your life by manifesting every positive dream.

> Let the Holy Spirit of God lead you for the rest of your life.

4.   Pray specifically and do not beat about the bush. So many people don't receive answers to their prayers because they have no clear objective

for their prayer. The bible says   "ask me, and I will give the heathen for your inheritance, and the uttermost parts of the earth for your possession". It is time to ask your heavenly Father to give you a proof of your dreams.

5.   Pray with Aggression and passion.
I have heard so many preachers say you do not have to shout for God to hear you, which is very true, but I also believe with all my heart that you need conviction when it comes to prayer. Conviction breeds aggression and passion, and it makes you to know who you are, and in whom you have   believed.

Conclusion

I want to encourage you as a prominent dreamer to keep growing into total maturity in the things of God. For if there is hope for a tree that is planted in a forest that if it be cut off, at the smell of water it shall sprout out again, then, there is hope for you! Rise up, you belong to the top, take your rightful place NOW!

"I have fought a good fight, I have finish my course, I have kept the faith, henceforth, there is laid up for me a crown of righteousness which the Lord, the righteous Judge, shall give me at that day and not to me only, but unto all them that love HIS appearing." Jesus is coming sooner than you think, do you love His appearing? Will you make it to heaven? Are your sins forgiven? Have you accepted Jesus as your Lord and personal saviour of your life? Is your

Dear Lord Jesus, have mercy on a sinner like me, come into my life, make me born again, and write my name in the book of life, I repent, amen!

name written in the book of life?

He wants to give you an opportunity to sincerely answer yes to all the questions above. Please pray this shot prayer with me: Dear Lord Jesus, have mercy on a sinner like me, come into my life, make me born again, and write my name in the book of life, I repent, amen!

You have just been accessed to the born again experience. Locate a very good bible believing, spirit filled church close to you and serve the Lord with all your heart, you will never regret it!

Do not die yet, stay alive, and make an impression for Christ! In Jesus Name, Amen!

NOTE

NOTE

NOTE

NOTE

NOTE